A Collection of Christmas Stories

Journey
through the
Christmas Chaos

Shelly D. Templin & Laura Reimer

CONTENTS

INTRODUCTION

In the fall of 2017, Laura decided to step way out of her comfort zone and attended a writer's conference held annually in Dallas, Texas. Before one of the sessions, she sat alone at a table, hoping for the chance to make some connections. She was joined by another attendee who was visibly upset. Shelly was usually a sunny Texan, but that day, she carried a burden for one of her own. Soon, two blonde heads were bowed in prayer as current family situations for both were lifted up.

As they departed the conference, they exchanged their "business cards" and promised to stay in contact. Shelly and Laura reconnected through emails in the following months and decided to attend the conference the following year. Two other gals joined them that year, and when they left the conference, the group of four agreed they wanted to stay in contact to encourage one another in their writing, speaking, and podcast endeavors. The messages between the four flew back and forth for the next few weeks. Then, Shelly and Laura realized it was just them.

Shelly and Laura's friendship continued to grow long-distance through texts and many, many Marco Polo conversations that could go viral simply based on their wild morning hair, readers perched on their noses, and the mutual love they have for all things tender and funny. Oh yes, and more prayer. It is a rare find in the writing community to be kindred spirits, yet each has a unique voice. Both writers view their everyday circumstances with an eye for how God might be speaking a word for us all. With humor and sensitivity to the bittersweet nature of change, each brings a personal perspective, often leaving readers feeling understood.

Shelly started a blog called Chuckles in the Chaos in 2012, and Laura has been blogging about her Journey Onward since 2013. Their material comes from their active and growing families, observations from daily life, and a mutual love for encouraging others.

This collection of Christmas musings and stories is a gift to all those who love the holidays but are ready to put their feet up and sip coffee in a quiet space when it's all wrapped up!

Sincerely,

Shelly & Laura

DON'T CRY OVER SPILLED GRAPE JUICE

Shelly

To say Christmas was a big thing in my family growing up is a huge understatement. HUGE. When Hubby and I were engaged, I thought it would be a good idea to take him home with me for Christmas so he couldn't claim I didn't warn him after we were married.

My family did NOT disappoint. My Dad met us as we exited the plane in a **green and white** Santa suit! My nephews might have been wearing reindeer antlers. That was in the days before 9/11 when whole families would wait for someone to get off the plane. And my entire family did!

He was warned. And he married me anyway.

Christmas at my house always included a "program." It started innocently enough. I was looking for a way to keep my little girls and nephews out of the kitchen so my mom could do her Christmas cooking prep. I kept them busy creating a show with costumes and songs. We depleted my mom's cotton ball supply so we could glue them to paper plates to make lamb face masks. We raided the brown paper bag stash to make donkey heads. My nephews were the cutest manger animals. My littlest girl was a precious "Mary."

That was the first year. As the kids grew, the program changed but always someone sang, played an instrument, acted out a play or did a dance. Or two.

One year, we decided to have Christmas Eve at home. We gathered in the formal living room, where twinkling Christmas lights created a festive atmosphere. My young nephew plunked out a few Christmas carols on the piano, we sang a few more songs, and my dad prepared to read the Christmas story. Can you just envision the lovely Norman Rockwell scene?

The plan was to take communion. The whole family was sitting either on the almost white carpet or the mostly white couches. My mom filled a silver goblet with grape juice and had bread ready. What happened next is a blur. Some aspects of it are very clear. Very.

I'm unsure how the grape juice got out of the goblet and all over the primarily white carpet and couches - yes, plural. Both of them.

I can't remember if it was a dog, a child, an adult, or some other force. But I do remember my mom shrieking and my dad using the closest word to cussing he ever said. DANGNABBIT!

Everyone jumped up. Mom ran for water, stain spray and cloths. We all went into operation **"save the carpet and couches"** mode. Dangnabbit might have been uttered again.

Thirty minutes later, the couches were too wet to sit on, my nephews had moved on to play a game and everyone's attitudes stunk. Christmas Eve was ruined.

Or was it?

We moved into the living room and gathered around to try again. I'm not sure which parent insisted we try again, but we did. I don't think anyone actually said, "We *WILL* have our Christmas Eve communion or else" but it was close to that.

After a few minutes, we calmed down and focused on the reason why we were trying to have communion on Christmas Eve – other than no one was capable of singing a moving rendition of *Oh, Holy Night* as we lit candles.

Seriously, Christmas Eve marks the birth of our Savior, Jesus. As Christians, we are eternally grateful for the birth of Jesus. But without what he did 33 years later on the cross, the birth wouldn't be significant. Communion is the time we stop and acknowledge that the baby, Jesus, born on Christmas grew up and willingly gave His life for all humanity so we can have eternal life.

Jesus told Him, *"I am the way, the truth, and the life. No one can come to the Father except through me." John 14:6*

It took time, effort, and a lot of stain spray, but eventually, we took time to remember and reflect on our gratitude for Jesus's birth and death.

How do you focus on the true meaning of Christmas?

Are there things you need to let go of or lay aside so you can focus on the birth of Jesus?

NOW DO IT
SOME MORE

Laura

At some point in my adult journey, someone was listening to me complain about my failed attempts at some project and interjected, with concerned counsel, about the need to overcome my perfectionism.

I responded with exasperation that she was obviously not listening to a thing I just said because clearly, I was the farthest thing from perfect that you could get. Did she not just hear how short I had fallen on my expectations for myself?????

While I can't remember which long-suffering friend it was who confronted me with this, I do remember her eyes just blinking at me for several long seconds until I said....oh.

I want to do all things well.

And by well, I mean the standard I have deemed to be excellent for a given task. No matter what the task is, the bar is set high in my mind.

So, I meticulously fold the laundry the way I think it should be folded and load the dishwasher the way I think it should be loaded and you name it.

I have my criteria for what is acceptable and if I am rushed and decide that 80% perfect is what I am going to have that day, then I can mark off another task done as done correctly. But for the rest of the day I will beat myself up over how I could have done it better.

When I taught classes at church, I didn't want to see the evaluations at the end of the session. Any mark less than the highest was devastating. If 6 was excellent than a 5 on any point meant I failed the whole thing.

To me there is no "constructive criticism." It's all destructive.

Now before you lecture me, please hear this. Many of you do not struggle with perfectionism and that is cool. You have a quick answer for people like me. So perhaps you need to walk a mile in my shoes, which took me quite a while to select this morning because I wasn't sure what would look right with this particular pair of jeans.

This is an unhealthy, pre-programmed issue in me that, thanks be to God, He is working out of me year after year. But it is something I struggle with overcoming, just like others of you struggle with your natural wiring.

While I battle it year-round, Christmas is a particularly difficult season. I have set up in my mind just how I want the house to look, the meals to turn out, the presents to be wrapped and the receiver of each gift to be pleased and feel loved and seen.

It's a lot of pressure on me, but also on everyone around me to meet and exceed my expectations. Social media has fueled these to a level that even surpasses my creative excess, and it is all a set up for disappointment and regret.

There is a passage of Scripture that I have found helpful in fighting this inner battle with my perfectionist seeking ways.

> *Brothers and sisters, we taught you how to live in a way that will please God, and you are living that way. Now we ask and encourage you in the Lord Jesus to live that way even more.*
> *1 Thessalonians 4:1*

Now, if I read this at the bottom of my performance evaluation, I might read it as something like this:

Laura, you have learned the things we taught you that are pleasing to God and we are so blessed to see how you are doing them. You are living the very things we taught you. Good job. Now do it better.

What?

I am meeting the expectation, but I need to improve? Already my stomach is in a knot.

I missed the mark? I want details. What didn't I do well enough? I have a good excuse. Let me explain…Give me another chance.

Ha! The litany of the Perfectionist! I know it well!

But instead, God is showing me here that pleasing Him is not a check list to be performed on a grading scale.

I am not being evaluated. I am being **commended** and **encouraged**. Exhorted, if you will.

I have learned some things about how to walk with Jesus and I have made the commitment to do it every day. This is good. So today, I will do it some more.

And as I follow His teachings, I will be stretched to apply them to new levels…day after day…one step at a time.

It's a journey, not a destination. Therefore; journey onward, my friends, in the ways you have been taught that are pleasing to God. Then; do it some more.

Keep doing it.

Day after day.

Heavenly Father, as I try to create a celebration of this season that honors you and blesses the people I love, help me to stop striving for a level of perfection that I have created in my own mind. Help me to set realistic goals that allow me time to enjoy our family, and provide quiet spaces to simply meditate on the joy of Christmas this year. Quiet any voices of comparison that would drive me to do more than I am capable of. Remind me daily that the way You sent your Son into the world was far from perfect according to the standards of earth, but absolutely perfect for your Kingdom. In Jesus' Name, Amen.

SNOWMEN NOSES
AND CHRISTMAS CHEER

Shelly

When I first married, I started a Santa collection. It didn't take me long to figure out there wasn't a lot of variety when it came to Santas. They were all pretty much wearing red suits trimmed in white fur and were fat with a long beard and twinkling eyes. So, I switched my collecting efforts to snowmen - and snow women and snow boys and snow girls.

I have snowmen made out of square blocks and ice cubes. I have snowmen standing on their heads, roasting marshmallows, and decorating a moose with Christmas lights. I have snowmen with skis and snowmen with shovels. Some snowmen blink, and others flicker. I even have a snowman dressed like a Santa.

Each year, when the time comes to pack away the Christmas decorations, these carefully selected snowmen pose a bit of a challenge. The Santas are easy – I just have to alternate their plump bodies in the box. Even though the snowmen come in all shapes and sizes, that is not what challenges my packing skills. It's their noses. All of the snowmen have one thing in common – carrot noses that **stick out.**

As I carefully pack away the snowmen, I have to arrange them so as not to smash any of their noses. What a pity it would be if next December, when I opened the "snowman" box, none of them had noses.

Last year, as I was arranging and rearranging the snowmen and their noses, I thought to myself (or maybe I mumbled it), "We wouldn't want any of you to get your noses bent out of shape."

Noses bent out of shape. Webster defines this term as "getting upset, agitated, or angry."

I thought about all of the noses in our family that get bent out of shape for one reason or another during the celebratory Christmas season. *We often work so hard to do things for our family that we frequently forget to consider them.* Ouch!

I know that I am guilty of getting so busy with decorating

~ and shopping
~ and present wrapping
~ and Christmas card sending
~ and baking
~ and cooking,

that I often get agitated and upset. My nose gets bent out of shape.

But this year, as I look at the snowmen around my house, they are more than just cute figures. They have a new meaning. They are a reminder for me. A reminder not to let my nose get bent out of shape.

My snowmen can remind me of the true meaning of this season – the birth of our Lord, Jesus.

And there were shepherds living out in the fields nearby, keeping watch over their flocks at night. An angel of the Lord appeared to them, and the glory of the Lord shone around them, and they were terrified. But the angel said to them, "Do not be afraid. I bring you good news that will cause great joy for all the people. Today in the town of David a Savior has been born to you; he is the Messiah, the Lord. This will be a sign to you: You will find a baby wrapped in cloths and lying in a manger." Suddenly a great company of the heavenly host appeared with the angel, praising God and saying,

"Glory to God in the highest heaven, and on earth peace to those on whom his favor rests."
Luke 2:8-14

Does your nose ever get bent out of shape during the Christmas season?

What are ways you can keep your focus on the birth of Jesus?

YOU ARE HIS PEOPLE

Laura

When our grandchildren were little, we looked forward to an annual pre-holiday trek to a reindeer ranch about an hour from our house. Our daughter found it on the internet one year and suggested we meet up there. It was so much fun we made it an annual event until the oldest boys got involved in sports and free time on the weekends dwindled away.

Watching the little ones cavort on the hay bales and playground area as we waited our turn was a photographic feast for this grandma who snaps pictures like she's filming a documentary. There was a cafe with ample tables set up for hot chocolate, cookies and even a BBQ lunch basket if you were so inclined. Gaudy Christmas decorations abounded along with a collection of vintage farm equipment.

The gift shop was a must-see for everyone, although some years it was dicey. Four sets of small hands and big curiosity are a dangerous combination. It was man-to-man defense as we navigated the shelves of knickknacks and ornaments. When one of our cherubs broke something, we learned the painful lesson about purchasing and then throwing away the shards of glass.

Our visit always seemed to happen on the coldest day of the month. I probably could have bought a fairly nice North Face jacket for what we spent on gas, lunch and tickets for the "Reindeer Experience."

But I can tell you, I would have pawned all my coats and a couple of pairs of mittens just to see their sweet faces as those amazing animals came right up and ate out of our hands.

Because they are my people.

They are worth far more than any amount of cash I could ever tuck away in a bank account. To love them and know them and spend time with them; to think about them all the time, along with their parents and our other offspring is my heartbeat on planet Earth.

Oh sure; I care about a lot of people, but these - these are my flesh and blood. So, when I think of Jesus, I think about how He had a special love for His people.

Oh yes, He came to save the world, but in John 17 we see the depth of Jesus' heart for some who were close to Him and I can relate to this.

As Jesus is in the Garden of Gethsemane, He is pouring out prayers. And in this passage Jesus is praying for His own people: the ones who loved Him as well as us selfish, goofy, flawed humans can grasp love.

I pray for them. I am not praying for the world, but for
those you have given me, for they are yours.
John 17:9

I am not praying for those who are of the world.

It's not that He didn't come to save all of us; but as He is finishing it all out, He is praying for His people.

Because there were others who didn't love Him.

They didn't choose Him.

They didn't want to be part of Him and so they were not part of Him.

So, as He prayed in the Garden, He wasn't being mean. He was just praying for the ones who were His.

He was praying for the ones who had traveled with Him, who had "done life with" Him and who had recognized that He was from God and believed He was Messiah. And even if they didn't get it right all the time, they were willing to hang in there and learn some more when they messed up.

So today, if you are spending time with your people...your family by blood...your family in the Blood... friends that have found such a deep place in your heart that you may as well share the same DNA... and you are loving them so much that sometimes it almost hurts...

remember…

YOU…

You are HIS people.

He is praying for you.

He loves you with that intensity and more...and He loves you perfectly.

Rest in the truth that if you have believed in Him and have believed HIM...

YOU ARE HIS PEOPLE...

Rest well in that today .... deer.

Father God, thank You for making someone like me a part of your family. Thank You for your love for me through your Son, Jesus Christ. Thank You for the love You have given me for my earthly family, by blood and by choice and by faith. Lord, help me to love with Your love. Help me to love the unlovely with the same passion that I have for those who are so dear to me. Only You love perfectly. Perfect Your love in me. I ask in Jesus' Name, Amen

YOU CAN DRESS
THEM UP BUT...

Shelly

Imagine a young mom flying without her husband across the country at Christmastime with two little girls. Imagine that young mom is me – or was.

When my girls were little, I traveled from Texas to my parents' home in Boise, Idaho twice a year with the girls - sans Hubby. I wanted to go "home" the day they got out of school and stay until they went back so that meant I had to wrangle the girls on a plane by myself. And this was before the days of iPads and other gadgets to keep them occupied. Just me, the girls and their little backpacks filled with toys of their choice.

Since the airports were busy, I dressed them in matching outfits so they'd be easier to keep track of and hopefully garner sympathy from others as I herded them through the airports. At Christmastime, I usually made us matching outfits to save money, and in the 90's, that's what moms did. DIY and crafting shows were brand new, so we tried to become experts at puff paint and anything else that involved paint and an iron. One year, I made cute Christmas vests for my girls that they wore with a turtleneck and leggings.

On the plane from Houston to Denver, my most wiggly daughter asked for a Sprite in a cup. I knew it was a bad idea, but I also knew the fight she would give me would be worse. So, after providing all the warnings and directions about sitting still and not bumping her tray, I let her have a cup.

Note: For you youngster moms reading this, you need to know we didn't have the newfangled bottles like Hydro Flasks. We had sippy cups until they drank out of regular cups. We didn't travel with our personal bottles with pop-up straws. For you moms my age, can I get an Amen?

I let my 6-year-old have a plastic cup of Sprite—against my better judgment. It didn't take but about 90 seconds for my wiggly daughter to bump the tray and send her whole cup of ice and Sprite into her seat—on her and under her. I immediately went into Supermom mode and mopped up all the spilled drink I could.

Wiggly daughter was not happy her pants were soaked. I wasn't happy either.

Thankfully, we landed soon, and we went straight to the restroom. We had a two-hour layover and another two-hour flight so I was on a mission to get the pants dry.

Now imagine a pregnant mom standing in an airport bathroom with a pile of carry-on bags on the floor, a 4 year old with her thumb in her mouth silently watching and another little girl standing as close to her mom as possible with her turtleneck shirt pulled down to dress length so her panties didn't show while the mom held her leggings under the hand dryer.

It's a good thing I had them dressed in cute matching Christmas vests. Ha! We were a sight.

Women came in and out. They glanced our way. Some looked embarrassed, and some looked sympathetic. Merry Christmas!

At that moment, I was an exasperated mom. I wanted to show up at my mother's house with my daughters cutely dressed. Instead, I arrived tired and flustered with a sticky-legged, soggy-pants daughter. But we were together for Christmas (Hubby arrived a few days later). Clothes can be washed, and naps cure a multitude of ailments - like grouchy attitudes.

As we hustle and bustle around this holiday season, can I encourage you to take the time to remember what is important? Take time to remember why we put up a tree or set out the menorah, buy presents, and gather with loved ones. Concentrate on what IS important and let go of what isn't.

My reason: Jesus

For a child is born to us, a son is given to us.
The government will rest on his shoulders.
And he will be called: Wonderful Counselor,
Mighty God, Everlasting Father, Prince of Peace.
Isaiah 9:6

As you hustle and bustle, remember to reflect on the Son of God, who was born to save us.

O CHRISTMAS TREE

Laura

Over the years, we have wavered between live and artificial trees. When we finally owned our home as a young couple, I wanted us to have the traditional tree farm experience. As we ventured amongst the evergreens, looking for the perfect tree, I would even imagine - with dewy eyes- someday introducing our children to this holiday tradition.

It didn't pan out the way.

There was the year we were frozen to the bone and thankful to be almost done with the task. As we stood at the counter ready to pay, I discovered the checkbook had fallen out of my pocket somewhere... out there. There was no humor whatsoever as we tromped back through the rows of pines on frostbitten feet until someone else told us a checkbook had been turned in at the office.

The years of discovering crooked trunks, large gaps between branches that had gone unnoticed, and a discrepancy between the diameter of the stem and our tree stand eventually took its toll on us.

After a particularly grim outing with two small children in tow, I buried the dream and bought an artificial one.

I realized the tree farm tradition was not meant for us. But God had bigger plans. After a couple of years that allowed for space and healing, Russ suggested we get a live tree. He did add the caveat that we needed to forego the tree farm and instead visit local vendors.

We were happy with the compromise and learned to take the tree stand with us to eliminate unpleasant surprises. Our new tradition morphed even more as Russ was busy at work and the kids' extracurricular kept us on the go from morning til night.

One year, we had a plan in place before things went slightly awry, making the checkbook fiasco look mild.

On a brisk day in early December, I set out with a list of things to do. One of my tasks was to scout out trees at a couple of the lots and then we would go back and pick it up when Russ got off work. We had only that evening to get a tree home as the rest of the week was booked.

So, with good intentions to stay on task, I headed out to run errands and assess trees.

As I checked off several items, I got the bright idea to go out to the local tree farm we had visited back in the old days and get a fresh-cut tree. Blame it on sleep deprivation or carb overload, but I soon found myself shivering in gale-force winds. I had not worn a coat to run errands in town. All I had for warmth was a hooded sweatshirt I had thrown on in the parking lot of the Four E's Trees parking lot.

Having greatly underestimated the wind chill out in the country, I faced an army of fresh-cut evergreens leaning against fence railings close to the car park. This was a bonus as my teeth were chattering and I had lost interest in attempting to explore the rows of live trees waiting to be cut.

Eventually, I was joined by a tree guy encased in Carhart from head to toe, with only his eyes and part of his mouth visible. We made an odd couple as he held out trees, and I sized each one with my arms bowed out like a ballerina because that's how I had measured the space available in our family room corner.

After quite a few attempts, we found a winner. Another thermally disguised guy bailed it and slid it into the trunk. Unfortunately, there was just about a foot of the tree that was too long to close the lid.

He offered me a bucket 'o twine with which to secure the hatch and his apologies that he could not fasten it for me, nor help, because they didn't want to be liable for any damage if something happened on the way home.

Can I tell you, this was my first indication that perhaps I was treading in waters where someone like me should not be?

But it was too late.

I was committed, and the Carhartt team disappeared to help the next naive housewife who had ventured out alone on a weekday.

I fastened the trunk lid down, and the manner in which the process occurred will be forever a secret because what happens at the tree farm stays at the tree farm. Suffice it to say that the tree, the trunk of the car, and I arrived home safely, in spite of potholes, railroad tracks, high winds, and the open door alert that sounded the entire 20-minute ride.

As I hoisted the tree onto the porch, I thought I heard the distant strains of Helen Reddy singing, "I am Woman, Hear me Roar." Ha!

I have to be honest. In my mind, every year, I carry this lovely vision of the family outing to pick a tree. But over the years the ONLY tradition is that, at some point, we did get a tree home or hauled up out of the basement. And often it made for a good story, eventually.

Often, we have expectations attached to the events around the holidays that have nothing to do with the point of why we do it. We listen to other families' stories, see commercials depicting houses, watch Christmas movies, and surf the internet.

Somehow, our version of preparing for Christmas just doesn't seem to be the right way. We remember, with rose-colored glasses, Christmas past and sigh and long for those better days, forgetting they were no more perfect than today is!

Really, the only "wrong" way to celebrate Christmas is to lose sight of why we do any of these things.

We are celebrating the birth of the One who came to save us from ourselves...from our sins...Emmanuel...God with us... The Prince of Peace... The Sovereign Lord...come to think of it: the Lion of Judah...hear HIM roar!

As we go about the preparations for this season, let us ever be mindful that at the center of it all is the coming of our Savior. God bless you as you let that joy fuel all your efforts.

Heavenly Father, as I live in the tension between the temporal and the eternal... as I place trinkets that remind me of the traditions of our own childhood, the years we raised our children, dear friends and family; O Lord let me not forget. These things are the gifts of this life, and while they warm my heart and provide the scenery for my journey here on earth...they are temporal. Let the Cross be ever before me...that my eyes would not be led astray by the things of this earth. Lord, lift my eyes above this season to the purpose of Christ's coming. And Lord, fill me with Hope for His blessed Return.

PIECES OF SANTA

Shelly

My husband and I were traveling to a different state for a college football game. We were touring the town's quaint square, which was filled with shops and restaurants. Even though it was only October, when my daughter spotted a "unique" Santa figurine that looked like it needed to be added to my collection, I bought it.

The salesgirl wrapped it up (and I use the term "wrapped" very loosely) and put it on the bottom of the bag. I had wandered off during Santa's bagging and had no idea that it was at the bottom of the bag, so the next day, when I slung the bag of "clothes" into the truck, I heard a *thump*.

I later found out that the thump was Santa's boots breaking off.

When we returned home and unpacked, I left Santa and his boots lying on the kitchen counter since I knew I had several weeks to deal with my crippled St. Nick. It wasn't urgent.

I left the house to run some errands, and when I returned, I saw a bottle of Super Glue lying next to Santa, and one of his boots was attached. My husband, bless his heart, knows I love my little Santas, so he sweetly tried to glue Santa back together. I was grateful my husband was trying to help me, so I let him tackle the project. Later that night, the other boot was attached.

But there was bad news. Santa could no longer stand up!

"Didn't you glue the boots back on just like they were?" I asked.

"I thought I did. But then I found these two little pieces. I didn't think they would make that much of a difference because they were so small - but I guess they do. Maybe we can glue some felt onto Santa's heels." My husband replied.

"Well, we have some time to figure it out." And Santa was tucked away in a supine position until after Thanksgiving.

Just two little, tiny pieces. Just a few itty-bitty pieces were missing. And Santa could no longer stand.

I can relate. Can you?

A little bit of our life is broken and we fear we can no longer stand. Even when we try to patch up the broken parts, there is often something left out, missing, that makes us unstable.

Maybe it's the death of a loved one. A missing piece.

Maybe it's an abuse that was committed against you that took a piece of your innocence.

Maybe it's words that were spoken about you or over you that caused a piece of your confidence or self-worth to fall away.

Maybe it's a decision you made that cost you a piece of your integrity.

Missing pieces. Itty-bitty, missing pieces that make us think we will never be able to stand again. And maybe we can't. Not on our own.

But the good news is that there is a Heavenly Father that makes all things new. He can turn our sorrow into dancing. He can give us joy and hope in our despair. He can strip off our grave clothes so that we can be truly free.

Then He who sat on the throne said,
"Behold, I make all things new." And He said to me,
"Write, for these words are true and faithful."
Revelation 21:5

Do not sorrow, for the joy of the Lord is your strength.
Nehemiah 8:10

You have turned my mourning into joyful dancing.
You have taken away my clothes of mourning
and clothed me with joy.
Psalm 30:11

Jesus called in a loud voice, "Lazarus, come out!"
The dead man came out, his hands and feet wrapped with strips
of linen, and a cloth around his face Jesus said to them,
"Take off the grave clothes and let him go."
John 11:44

Whatever piece you are missing, know that Jesus heals our physical, emotional and spiritual wounds so that we can stand. And stand strong.

I will declare that your love stands firm forever,
that you have established your faithfulness in heaven itself.
Psalm 89:2

Dear Lord, take our broken pieces and help us to stand. Thank you for sending your Son to earth to die for us so that we can have eternal life and have abundant life here on earth.

IT REALLY IS
A JOURNEY

Laura

At the holidays, we hustle about and exert energy into pulling off a perfect Christmas. Yet, in the quiet moments, as we attempt to drift off to sleep, the heart can be tender for those navigating difficult settings during what should be the most wonderful time of the year, as the song goes.

Many can be hard-pressed during the holiday season, and yet others are experiencing great bounty. If our hearts are open to the journeys of others, we can feel pulled in many directions emotionally.

Whatever your season of life, we share the good and the hard times in fellowship, partaking of both with love, grace, and thanksgiving to God. Be assured that you are loved and cared for, and you matter much to God!

I remember one year when we were on all ends of the spectrum of life. The Wednesday before Thanksgiving, Russ and I got to attend Grandparent's Day at our firstborn grandson's preschool.

Let me tell you, the little guy was bountifully blessed that day. Among all the other wonderful things he had going for him, four doting grandparents were in attendance for the festivities.

I do not boast in us as grandparents... I can only say that I would have loved the opportunity to have my own grandparents close by and to have known them the way this little guy and his siblings have known theirs!

There is a lot of life and history with the four of us who raised his parents. Over the years, we have driven his mommy and daddy to dances and ball games before they could drive, chaperoned youth events together, and now love and pray for this next generation that shares our genes and fills our hearts.

So, on our visit to his school, we stood huddled together, beaming over every little thing he did. We took turns making handprints for a picture, sharing the list of questions we were given to ask about his day, getting photos with him, and squeezing into tiny little chairs at all the various stations around the room.

It was an action-packed hour, and by the time it was winding down, the room was well-used. Near the end, I went over to the craft area to help with clean up.

As I gathered glue and scissors, my ears perked up as the young teacher asked a woman, who appeared to be a great-grandma, if she was having people in for Thanksgiving. When I heard the older woman sigh and hesitate, I looked up and made eye contact with her.

According to our oldest daughter, this would be the reason I get drawn into people's stories...it's the eye contact.

Sure enough, she began to speak to me and the teacher, explaining how she used to have everyone to her house, but the mantle had been passed to her daughter. As she shared, her eyes started to fill with tears. So did mine, and so, there we stood amidst the scraps of construction paper, three women from three generations:

- One young teacher who has recently disclosed she is expecting her first child.
- Me in the early stages of being a grandma.
- One great-grandma who now looks back over it all with the wistful eyes of one who has served well.

I told her I understood her sorrow and that I, too, love the role of preparing for family to return to their homestead.

It is a joy to prepare the food and have the house filled with loved ones. I also struggle with changes that have come with a grown-up family, and I know my time doing this is really for a season. So, the thought of that season coming to an end someday adds a touch of bittersweet to the holidays.

I searched for a word to describe how I feel as time marches on, and finally, I looked her in the eye and said, "Sometimes, I feel displaced."

Yes, yes...that was it...she said as she nodded her head.

"I feel displaced."

And so, the younger woman with all of it still ahead, the older woman with all of it behind, and me somewhere in the middle: we had a moment.

Three generations and we were suddenly painfully aware that life is a series of changes to which we must learn to adjust.

Whoever said, "The more things change, the more they stay the same," was not talking about family dynamics.

Life is a constant ebb and flow of change: children grow up, people pass away, friendships are lost, relationships struggle, babies are born, new friends are made, marriages add relatives, divorces take them away and in the midst of it all, we sometimes feel our footing shift, and it seems we may not make it through the current shaking.

We fear we will be so displaced that we will have been replaced when things fall into their new place.

And there are no guarantees on that.

The promises of God are not that we will be protected from the discomforts of change, but that He remains unchanged in the midst of all the great shiftings and losses and gains of life.

That He will comfort us in them.

That there is more to this life than our living day to day.

He is the same...yesterday...today...forever.

This life is temporal. He is eternal.

In all the changes, He is the one thing that remains.

Steadfast.

Sure.

Strong.

Right.

True.

And that, according to Scripture, is what Christmas is all about.

Jesus Christ, the Son of God, displaced Himself from glory to replace us on the cross so that we would have a place with Him in eternity.

The longer I live, the more I see that despite all the changes, He is our constant.

Wonderful Counselor

Mighty God

Everlasting Father

Prince of Peace

Wherever you are having to adjust today to the shiftings of time, I hope you are firmly standing on the eternal and unchanging love and grace of God given through the gift of His Son Jesus Christ.

God bless you and keep you today and throughout this season.

Heavenly Father, Thou knowest. Such words have kept me at times when the change of seasons has caught me off guard. Thou knowest my inmost thoughts. Thou knowest the passage of time that seems to have flown far more quickly than I was prepared for. Thou knowest how, at times, I feel displaced as our grown children find their wings. Thou knowest, the echoes in my heart as the house seems far to quiet and yet, I rejoice for the new places our children have found to call home. Help me find my rest and joy in You and You alone.

TEMPORARY CHRISTMAS

Shelly

When I was ten years old, my family of six, plus a dog, moved from the South to the Pacific Northwest. We left our big home where each kid had our own room and a big backyard. There were some delays in getting into our new house, so we moved into a home where we shared rooms, and the yard was about the size of a card table. The cramped quarters living arrangement was supposed to be temporary but lasted 18 months. After a few months, my teenage sister used tape to make a line down the middle of our room and told me I could only cross to get something out of our closet quickly. But that's probably a story for another day – or not.

Because we were only supposed to be in the temporary home... temporarily, most of our things were in storage. That proved challenging as Christmas approached. My mom didn't have a roasting pan for the turkey. She wanted to bake banana bread to give as gifts but didn't have loaf pans, so everyone got a coffee tin-shaped loaf that year. The Christmas tree and ornaments were stored away.

My parents put a positive spin on our Christmas décor dilemma. We

We would have an old-fashioned Christmas! Off to the tree lot we went to get a real tree.

Harkening back to days gone by, we strung popcorn and cranberries as garland for the tree. I drew my best 5th grader star on a white paper plate. My brother cut it out, and I covered it with aluminum foil. My dad taped it to the top of the tree. We wrapped a sheet around the tree's base as our makeshift tree skirt- a far cry from the sequined skirt my grandmother made for my parents when they were newlyweds.

We stood back and admired our first handmade Christmas tree, and I think we are all proud of our accomplishments.

And the next day, we went to church.

When we came home, all of the popcorn-cranberry garland on the bottom half of the tree was **gone**! The little dog I won at Vacation Bible School (now, that's another story for another day) ate the garland!

That year, our tree only had decorations on the top half, but we didn't care. Presents still fit under it.

My family has a saying we coined during those 18 months – "Are we having fun or making memories?" ***Making memories*** was usually the unanimous response.

I often go into the holiday season with high expectations. Expectations about all I will accomplish. Expectations about all I will accomplish. Expectations of family time Expectations of cozy nights in front of a fire with family laughing and sipping cocoa while playing a game or working on a puzzle. Expectations of having enough money to buy the gifts. Expectations of making cookies and taking them to neighbors and friends.

My expectations are not always met. Usually, they aren't. But those things are not what makes Christmas...Christmas. Christmas is remembering the importance of a baby boy being born to save mankind. I often must work hard to remember why I decorate, bake, gather, and shop, even though a creche is in my entryway and Christ-centered ornaments fill my tree.

No matter what ornaments we have or don't have to adorn our trees – or even if we have a tree or gifts under it, Jesus was still born over 2000 years ago. That is the most important expectation of all.

May you take time to let the expectations fall away and focus on remembering the birth of our Savior. May the true meaning of Christmas permeate and dominate everything you do this Christmas season. May you pause at the wonder of a God who loves us so much He was willing to send His son to this world to become the ultimate sacrifice for each of us. May you remember the baby boy, born in a barn, who is called *"God with us."*

All right then, the Lord himself will give you the sign. Look! The virgin
will conceive a child! She will give birth to a son and will call him
Immanuel (which means 'God is with us').
Isaiah 7:14

THE EBB AND FLOW
OF TRADITIONS

Laura

As our children got older, traveling to visit family for Christmas was not possible. Due to extracurricular sports and rehearsals for various groups and all the other things that take over your life in middle and high school, our normal Christmas routine became settled and comfortable.

We attended our church's latest service on Christmas Eve, which meant we slept in longer on Christmas morning. Egg casserole and Monkey Bread were served as we opened our stockings. From there we moved to the tree for presents and a day of lounging as we explored our gifts and played games. Eventually we would clean up a little bit and put together a nice dinner. After dessert, we were back in our pjs for a family movie.

Our Christmas routine was lovely, but not destined to last as long as we hoped. One summer when our oldest was headed back to her sophomore year in college and our youngest was starting seventh grade, we inherited a large chunk of the previous generation on my side of the family.

My father was deep in the throes of Alzheimers, my aunt was dealing with a hefty case of dementia and my mom, their caretaker, had succumbed to the stress of it all. She collapsed physically, emotionally and mentally.

We brought them all to our town, found the appropriate facilities for each one and watched our lives turn upside down in one fell swoop. Thankfully, my mom recuperated and we enjoyed the next five years with her fully engaged and renewed and restored to a better place than she had ever been.

My aunt and my dad were safe and cared for by people who could provide for their needs. And my husband and young family rose up to a level of kindness and grace and flexibility that still brings tears to my eyes decades later.

Among many things that looked different after we brought them into our circle was Christmas.

We still did the latest possible service on Christmas Eve and we still had our traditional breakfast/stockings and gifts. But the process had a time limit. Everyone knew that after a quick lunch we would pack up a cooler with Christmas treats, load the gifts for my parents and aunt, pick up my mom at her place and head to the nursing home where my aunt and dad lived.

Added to this was the bonus of my aunt's stepson, Jim, a bachelor from New York City whom our children had never met. Jim had lost

lost his father quite a few years before my aunt came to live with my parents, and he had continued to make an annual pilgrimage to see her at Christmas. When the holidays moved to our neck of the woods, entertaining Jim became a normal part of our "new" Christmas tradition.

We would all gather in the nursing home's family lounge. We would set up party plates and cups, holiday napkins and hand out the gifts. My dad, despite all the mental decline, still put a bow on his head, just as he had done every Christmas of my childhood. Conversation would circle around and around with very limited topics.

Our children would dutifully answer the same questions from my aunt and dad until we all were weary and could no longer carry on the repetitions without sounding irritated. We would pack up our things and say our goodbyes. Back home, everyone pitched in with helping me prepare dinner or visiting with Jim and my mom. Interestingly, I had never had so much kitchen help from all three before this turn of events.

The party would continue with dessert and a movie of some kind. This carried on for five years. Then we lost them, one by one. First my mom passed, just after Thanksgiving in 2008; followed by my aunt in the spring of 2009.

The next year, on the eve of my parents wedding anniversary, just three days before Christmas, I got a call. The nurse told me my father had taken a downward turn and was nearing the end of his life.

That morning, I set aside the massive Christmas To Do list. I put the brakes on everything that I had thought needed to be done. I sat next to my dad's bed at the nursing home most of the day.

One of our young pastors was delivering baskets from the church to the nursing home that day and ended up being one of the first people outside of family to know and share the day. Later a dear friend came with coffee and sat with me mostly in silence, talking when we needed to.

I was blessed to call our kids and hold the phone up so they could say goodbye.

I was blessed to do the same for my sister who had been estranged from him and she made her peace.

I was blessed to thank him for everything he had done for me and us and his family.

He hadn't been able to speak a word for at least a month and that day he just laid with his eyes closed breathing from the oxygen...but I know he heard us in his heart.

He had come to us seven years before in the ugly part of Alzheimer's.

It was rough, to say the least, and we learned the truth of why you find laughter in the worst situations; because the awful needs some balance.

I thank God for the support of my husband and children, our friends, our church and our sweet and kind God who gave me one last day to see my dad peacefully breathing. I sat beside him, quietly at rest before God took him Home.

He left us early the next day, as the morning dawned on what would have been another anniversary without his beloved wife.

Never doubt the kindness of God.

He is faithful.

In all the circumstances of life.

God bless you today as you treasure those you have, remember those who are gone...or grit your teeth and face the ugly of whatever you are dealing with...

God IS holding you and all you love because He IS love.

Father God, in all the seasons of my life, You have always been faithful. I have seen Your goodness to me and to my family in the hardest places. There have been times when it was in looking back that I was able to see, but always, always, You have been good and kind. As I have walked with You, I have learned to see that joy and sorrow mingle and that this is the story of the Cross. The birth of Your Son is a prelude to His death. Joy and Sorrow. And one day, only Joy. Help us to live with purpose as we wait for that day.

A FEW OF MY
FAVORITE THINGS

Shelly

When our three daughters were teenagers, we moved to a new town. We knew it was a hard time to make a move, so I was thrilled when my oldest daughter came home and asked to join an organization called Symphony Belles. The Belles handed out programs and ushered at the local symphony events and would also learn manners and leadership skills. We signed up and bought the LBD – Little Black Dress.

The Symphony Belles planned a Christmas party, but I wasn't aware of it until about 4 o'clock on a Sunday night – the night of the 6 o'clock party. Two hours before the party, a frantic daughter informed me she needed a Christmas ornament to take to the party for the exchange. And her friend needed one too.

We ran to Hallmark. Closed. Another store. Closed. And another. Closed. We were running out of time. As a last resort, I dashed into a Dollar General and got two $3 plastic ornaments that lit up with changing colors. To say my daughter was horrified that she (and her friend) would have to take such gaudy ornaments to a "high society' event is an understatement.

Just a little note: I prided myself on having emergency supplies on hand. I had cabinets stocked with folders, folders with pockets, folders with pockets and brads, folders without brads but with pockets, and an assortment of binders in different colors and sizes, poster board, construction paper, and even tri-fold poster board.

But Christmas ornaments weren't in my stash. They are now.

Back to the story.

My daughter wrapped up her ugly ornament and took off for the party hosted by one of the town's most well-known woman. HORRIFIED.

Guess what? When they did the ornament exchange, the two Dollar Store plastic ornaments were the ones the girls kept "stealing." High school girls had little use for Waterford or mercury glass ornaments. Blinking, rubbery ornaments were the rage.

My daughter was the Belle of the ball, I mean, party.

I am guilty of desiring a Pinterest-perfect Christmas. I want my home beautifully decorated, my tree trimmed exquisitely with all of our favorite ornaments, and the smells of Christmas wafting from my kitchen.

Most of our Christmas decorations were in storage two years ago while we lived in temporary housing. I didn't have my "big" Christmas tree, so we selected our favorite ornaments and hung them on a tiny tree. I didn't have space for my snowman or Santa collection to be on display, so I picked a handful of my favorites. There wasn't room for my fancy creche, so I displayed a miniature one I found in a local store.

When I think about that Christmas, I remember it fondly because our favorite things surrounded us. We gathered in our cozy living room to celebrate the birth of our Lord. We remembered that most holy night so long ago and gave thanks for the humble birth of Jesus.

The words to the familiar song "*O, Holy Night*" bring tears to my eyes when I absorb their meaning instead of just singing them. Have you ever focused on the words to the song? Will you, as you read them with fresh eyes?

O holy night! The stars are brightly shining;
It is the night of the dear Savior's birth.
Long lay the world in sin and error pining,
Till He appeared and the soul felt its worth.
A thrill of hope- the weary world rejoices,
For yonder breaks a new and glorious morn!
Fall on your knees! O hear the angel voices!

O night divine, O night when Christ was born!
O night, O holy night, O night divine!

Led by the light of faith serenely beaming,
With glowing hearts by His cradle we stand.
So led by light of a star sweetly gleaming,
Here came the Wise Men from Orient land.

The King of kings lay thus in lowly manger,
In all our trials born to be our Friend.
He knows our need— to our weakness is no stranger.
Behold your King, before Him lowly bend!
Behold your King, before Him lowly bend!

Truly He taught us to love one another;
His law is love and His gospel is peace.
Chains shall He break, for the slave is our brother,
And in His name all oppression shall cease.
Sweet hymns of joy in grateful chorus raise we;
Let all within us praise His holy name.
Christ is the Lord!
O praise His name forever!

His pow'r and glory evermore proclaim!
His pow'r and glory evermore proclaim!

May your Christmas be filled with all your favorite things, but mostly, the love and peace Jesus brings.

Waiting...waiting... waiting...

Laura

When our children were young, we would alternate Christmas morning between our parents homes. Occasionally a winter storm would change our plans and we might be at our own home or stuck at a hotel waiting for roads to be cleared.

Loving consistency, I desired to have some kind of "tradition" that we could have for Christmas morning that would remain the same, no matter our location.

Rachel had received a child-friendly nativity at her birth. Using this, I incorporated a sweet custom I had learned from a Catholic Church service in college. Attending on Christmas Eve, I discovered they leave the manger empty throughout Advent. Early on Christmas morning, the baby is added.

Since the pieces of her nativity were small, they could travel with us easily in a suitcase. The baby Jesus was wrapped in tissue and hidden somewhere in the house until Christmas morning. I was the only one who knew where it was, even when we were packed and on the road.

If I wanted to build a sense of anticipation...mission accomplished.

They drove me crazy as they got older trying to figure out where I had hidden the baby. One year, I hid him so well, I was afraid I wouldn't find him before they woke at the crack of dawn.

Another year, the absence was just too much. One morning in mid-December, I found the Mama Berenstain Bear figure from a Happy Meal in the manger.

She lay, as if in state, with her arms folded in front of her blue polka-dot dress, smiling kindly up into the faces of the holy family.

I laughed, but it made me think how we can get tired of waiting for Christ and decide to just fill in that place where He should be with something....anything... anyone...we can find.

While He always arrives perfectly on time, we can grow restless waiting.

Waiting for Him to change things, waiting for Him to heal, waiting for Him to provide what we think we need, waiting for Him to calm the storm, waiting for Him to make things right..and so we take matters in our hands.

And our results are, quite frankly, as ridiculous as a Mama Bear in a manger.

Even when we cannot sense His presence; He IS.....Immanuel...God with us.

Christmas is more than the tree, presents, baking, cards, parties and programs. It's more than the decorations and time with family.

The season of Christmas is a time of waiting. There is an anticipation of something significant and life-changing that gives us the hope that things can be better; that we can be better.

As we wait, it is so easy to fill that with things that simply don't belong in the place that only He can hold in our hearts.

This longing was what the people experienced when Jesus came the first time and it will be fulfilled in us when He returns.

Let's wait well together.

Heavenly Father, as the world waited for Messiah to come; we wait now for His return. We long for things to be made right and for His reign to be completed on earth. In the waiting, we grow weary and sometimes we are tempted to fill the space with other things that bring us comfort. Work in our hearts this holiday season to recognize the anticipation and longing in us is preparing us for His return. Even as we celebrate His birth, fill our hearts with Hope and Joy. Amen.

JOSEPH LOST
HIS HEAD

Shelly

Many years ago, I started a blog called Chuckles in the Chaos. I was in the throes of raising three teenage daughters with a husband who traveled for a living, so it felt like I was doing it alone. I wasn't, but it felt that way.

Oh, and the dogs. Dogs who ran up my vet bill, chased wild animals into the woods, or trapped them under our shed right as I was heading to bed. I started the blog to tell funny stories of our often chaotic lives and try to encourage others along the way, even if it only made you think your life wasn't so bad compared to my craziness.

Then, Covid hit, and life wasn't so funny. And Covid changed things - and me.

Well, I've moved and the next generation is giving me lots of chaotic things to chuckle about. And we've added a puppy (not mine, but she lives with me.) Wait, my 12-year-old deaf dog didn't start out as mine and he still lives with me. I digress.

If you think my life can't be that chaotic, let me give you a synopsis of my day.

Four-year-old grand-girl was dropped off at my house before I had poured the second cup of coffee. She scurried up the stairs and alerted me to dog poop. That was just the beginning of the poop pick-up. My dog is on meds for an infection that makes him poop more than a full-grown cow and pee more than seems possible. My daughter's pup is sick and her bowels are defiant. The poop pick-up count ended the day at 7. The pee clean-up count topped out at 4. Oh, and throw in 1 barf clean-up.

I know you are dying to visit my house now. Thank goodness for superior cleaning products.

Back to the grand-girl. We planned a special day with a trip to the American Girl Doll store at the fancy Dallas Galleria. She wanted to wear her new backpack doll carrier. Envision a three foot girl wearing a full size backpack and big doll hanging out of the backpack.

As soon as we crossed the threshold of the AGD store (that's what they call it...), it must have gotten heavy because she handed it to me. I carried it until our purchases were vying for space in my hands. Then I thought, "What the heck!" and put the pink backpack with a doll strapped in it on my back. No one in the AGD store gave me a second look.

We headed to the food court and I held my head high as I sported my doll backpack while passing the designer stores. Other grandparent-looking people gave me a quick nod of the head and a half smile that said, "We know. Good job."

There might have been a potty accident that caused me to dig through boxes in the garage to find a panty substitute for a four-year-old. The only thing I could come up with was a hand-me-down swimsuit from her sister. Did I tell you I moved, and most of my stuff is still in boxes?

So floral swimsuit and polka dot shirt were the fashion of the day. I had plans to hang garland on my porch railing but didn't want the judgment of my new neighbors. My old neighbors knew me well enough to know I normally wouldn't concoct such an outfit. Well, unless the Grand wanted to wear it. I'm the Nonna and don't have to do the clothes battles. I'll leave that to her mom. She owes me.

The day was chaotic yet full of joy, laughter, and dog tail wiggles. As I sat down after a long day, I looked over at the tiny creche on the end table and saw Joseph had lost his head. He might have had some help from a 4-year-old. Joseph's head was lying on the table near his feet. He was still standing with his staff near the manger but was headless.

I feel ya, man! I feel ya!

Often, in the busyness of the Christmas season, I get busy and run around like a chicken without my head. I focus on all the wrong things while trying to do all the right things. I function like Joseph sometimes. I'm physically in it but not all together in it.

This Christmas season, I vow to be more cognitive of what is important and not make myself weary with the things that are not. I want to keep my wits about me and focus on sharing the love of Jesus and the hope we have in Him.

But those who trust in the Lord will find new strength.
They will soar high on wings like eagles. They will run and not grow
weary. They will walk and not faint.
Isaiah 40:31

Here's to walking with a pink doll backpack - and not growing weary.

When you find yourself weary, stop and think of Mary in a barn holding her newborn son. The Promise. Let that image settle and calm you.

Away in a manger. No crib for a bed. The little Lord Jesus laid down His sweet head. The stars in the bright sky looked down where He lay. The little Lord, Jesus, asleep on the hay. The cattle are lowing. The Baby awakes, but little Lord Jesus, no crying He makes. I love You, Lord Jesus. Look down from the sky and stay by my side until morning is nigh. Be near me, Lord Jesus, I ask You to stay close by me forever and love me, I pray.

SCRUB TREES AND LIGHTS AND THE MAGIC OF CHRISTMAS

Laura

One year in early December, Russ and I stopped by our nearby grocery store and noticed the Boy Scouts were selling Christmas trees. Since we were in our "live tree, but not from a tree farm" phase of life, we pulled around after getting our groceries and selected a tree that looked like the right height and diameter.

When we got home, Russ got the tree in the stand and I began stringing the lights on the branches. My next task was to figure out what was the best looking side before I slid it into place to hang the ornaments. This proved challenging.

After circling the tree several times and looking at it from all angles, it became clear this tree simply did not have a good side. It was the oddest tree I had ever seen and why we hadn't noticed it before was a mystery.

But time was of the essence, so I just hung ornaments and shoved it back in the corner between the oversized chair and the piano and moved on.

Later in the week, Kyle, one of our son's friends was over. Since he was a Boy Scout, I asked him if they had evergreen branches for sale because I was getting ready to decorate the porch railing. Kyle assured me they had a great selection and then added that they cut them off of the scrub trees.

Scrub trees? I had never heard of such a thing so asked him what those were. He explained that some of the trees they get in aren't really shaped like traditional Christmas trees. Since no one wants those, they cut the branches off to make the garlands and stems they sell.

I am not always quick to connect dots, but even as Kyle was speaking I began to put the pieces together. To confirm my suspicions, I asked him to take a look at the tree in our living room.

Even bedecked with lights and trim, Kyle was able to immediately nod knowingly. Yes ma'am. That's a scrub tree. I couldn't help but laugh. Apparently in this transaction, both buyer and seller had been oblivious to the undesirable shape of this particular tree.

A few weeks later, I was dropping some cookies off at a neighbor's house in the early evening. Entering the foyer, I could see a glittering Christmas tree through an archway into their living room.

Having just stepped from the cold, damp December day into the warmth of this home, it caught my eye and I exclaimed how beautiful their tree was.

She laughed and said it was actually horrible looking. Worst tree ever. It only looked good when it got dark and they turned on the lights.

It sounded like our scrub tree with all the strings and wires visible between empty places, with an odd shape and mish-mash of ornaments, each with its own story. Kyle had seen it in the glare of the afternoon sun coming in our window, which accentuated all the imperfections.

But when night descended and we plugged it in...breathtaking.

And as I think about it, in our natural state we are not much different.

In the glaring light of day, with all our flaws and humanity hanging out there, we look pretty unremarkable. We actually are very much like the scrub trees. Not at all desirable really, when you take a good look at us. We are kind of rough around the edges and fall short of the mark most of the time.

But in the dark places; that's where the light of Christ shines brightest in us. It's where His love shines through us.

And we are transformed.

From ordinary to extraordinary.

Not because of *us*. No, it is His light in us that illuminates.

So shine on, dear one. The world is, indeed, dark and weary.

It is now, more than ever, that they need the Light, the Hope, the Spirit of Christ.

He IS Immanuel....God with US.

May God bless each of you this Christmas season and may the Light of His Life shine through each of you, transforming you from scrub to glory as only He can.

Father God, how often I have been reminded of my "scrub tree" nature. I am painfully aware of the places in me that are not beautiful. I feel odd and unwanted at times. At Christmas as we celebrate the birth of Your Son, I am reminded that He was described by the prophet Isaiah as being a bit of a scrub tree Himself. Yet it was because He had set aside His glory, Your glory, to come and walk among us. And it is His light and His life and His beauty that shine in me through my imperfections. Continue to work in me this season so that His light will brighten the darkness around me. Amen.

SINS AND SENSITIVITIES

Shelly

Christmas lists and Christmas gifts start filling my thoughts and notes each October. Sometimes, as I'm out and about running errands, I will find something I think one of my loved ones would enjoy getting as a gift. I purchase it and tuck it away—and hope I remember where I tucked it. I've been known to forget to give someone a tucked-away gift. My mom hid gifts really well, too, so I come by it naturally.

Sometimes I forget I've already bought a gift for someone and buy another one. Once, when that happened, I offered the gift to one of my daughters to give to her sister. It was a book I thought she would enjoy. I held the book out and said, "You want to give this to your sister?"

She backed away from it as if it were a serpent and violently shook her head, "NO!"

So, I wrapped up the book for the other daughter and put it under the tree. A gift from me.

Christmas holidays were always spent at my parents' house with all my siblings and their kids until about five years ago. It could get a little hectic with about 17 people gathered in the living room opening presents on Christmas morning, so it wasn't completely unusual when my sister came into the living room where we were all recovering from the Christmas dinner with an unopened gift – the book – and said she found it on the floor of her bedroom. Both of my girls looked like they wanted to fade into the couch they were sitting on.

I took the book and handed it to my daughter, saying, "This is for you." She said she didn't want it. How could she not want something when she didn't even know what it was?

There was a bit of confusion until I learned the story behind the discarded, unwanted gift.

As teenage sisters often do, my girls were known for behaving in a manner that often caused me to say, "You need to be more sensitive to your sister." I feel like I said it a lot. Probably to one daughter more than the other. Let's call that daughter, Sister A and the other one Sister B.

When I offered the book to Sister B to give to Sister A, she glanced at the title, and in her haste, she read it wrong. She knew Sister A would not want to be gifted a book by the title she thought was on the cover so when the book was handed to her, she warned her. Sister B whispered to Sister A, "You don't want to open that in front of everyone."

They opened the door to my sister's bedroom behind them and slid it in. In all the Christmas Chaos, we didn't see the slight of hand, er, book.

As my sister stood, holding the still-wrapped book, I tried to figure out what in the world was going on. I questioned why Sister B told Sister A she wouldn't want the book. We talked for a few minutes until we figured out what happened.

When Sister B looked at the book I offered her, she mistook the title as **Sins and Sensitivities** and there was *NO WAY* she was going to give *THAT* book to her sister. She thought it was a book about how teenagers should be more sensitive to each other. The book was the classic Jane Austen book _Sense and Sensibility_. And I thought Daughter A would like to read it.

Mystery solved. Confusion cleared up. Gift given and received.

Sometimes, we are like my daughters concerning the free gift of salvation we have through the sacrifice Jesus made for us on the cross —the reason He came to earth and was born in a stable filled with hay, animals, and probably...their waste. I'm just saying. Barns I have been in also had spiders, wasps, and other creepy, crawly things in them, so I imagine there were critters in the stable who witnessed the birth of our Savior.

For the wages of sin is death, but the free gift of God is
eternal life through Christ Jesus our Lord.
Romans 6:23

I know people who refuse to accept Jesus's gift of salvation because they think they will have to give up their freedom and be governed by a long list of rules. They miss out on the gift of grace and mercy. They miss out on the love, peace, and joy God offers to His children. Yes, there are some behaviors God wants us to steer clear of, but it's not because He's a giant fun-sucker. It's because He loves us and wants the very best for us and knows our human nature is full of sin and sometimes lacks sensibilities.

My daughters treated the classic Jane Austen book like a hot potato that would burn them and almost missed out on reading rich literature.

This Christmas season, I want to focus on the best gift ever given – Baby Jesus and the free gift of salvation he provided for us when he shed His blood on the cross. A sweet baby boy started out His life in a humble way and thirty-three years later ended it the same way.

Have you ever been reluctant to accept the gift of salvation or God's gift of love, joy, peace, grace, or mercy? Think about accepting the best gift of all this Christmas Season – Jesus as Lord and Savior.

But even greater is God's wonderful grace and his gift of righteousness, for all who receive it will live in triumph over sin and death through this one man, Jesus Christ.
Romans 5:17b

THE YEAR OF THE TROUBADOURS

Laura

I have been meditating on the feeling that comes over me as the days accelerate toward Christmas. It isn't anxiety because of any actual planned and choreographed event that is going to culminate on Christmas day. Based on our traditions, and the way those have been carried into our empty nest years, there isn't a lot of pizzazz to Christmas Day in our home.

When our three were still basically under one roof, our traditions involved an enthusiastic mom, a patient dad and children with various sleep habits. They had to wait until everyone was awake to come downstairs. I can still hear their voices as some begged for more time in bed while others danced around excitedly, lobbying to see what Santa had brought. And of course, for me, lots of coffee as the process played out each year.

While the egg casserole and Monkey Bread waited on the table, Russ would gather us to read the Christmas story from Luke. Then it was breakfast and stocking opening. After that, presents, more coffee, and just hanging out until we started putting the pieces together for the Christmas feast.

The years with the triplets (my mom, dad and aunt) in various facilities around town brought some changes as we incorporated a makeshift party at the nursing home into the afternoon. This meant we had to get dressed in real clothes. Not exactly a Martha Stewart scene or a spread for a decor magazine, but it worked for us.

Time has changed much of this considerably. The triplets are all gone. So are the three dancing children. They have jobs and homes and maybe that's why the days hurtling past are difficult.

We try to find a time when everyone can be together. Sometimes it happens and sometimes it just doesn't work. And that's okay.

Hard, but okay.

We raised them to be fruit-bearing, God-loving, Christ-celebrating adults. And they are. We just didn't know how loud the echoes would be sometimes and the holidays seem to intensify those.

So, we live deeper. We live richer.

We treasure the past in tender, hidden places in our hearts, so we can make room for the NOW. We have new voices that are filling our home. We have more days ahead to attempt to gather all together in one place. We enjoy who we are with, when we are with them - and we always miss the ones who are not there.

This place of quiet around the holidays is where some sweet

memories rise up. The Christmas after 9/11 was a bittersweet time for our nation. We were shaken and had a new kind of fear to manage when December rolled around that year. But children seem to have a way of changing our perspective.

That year, John, our youngest, was in the elementary band along with most of the boys who lived on our street. He cooked up the idea that instead of caroling, they would take their instruments house to house and try out some Christmas songs they were attempting to learn. Surprisingly, his buddies all agreed that this was a great idea. And so, on a cold winter evening, another mom and I walked with them to help carry stands and music.

Or, more accurately, we ran with them.

In a fashion that resembled more of a sporting event than a concert, they took the neighborhood by horn. What they lacked in skill, they made up for in volume and enthusiasm. Neighbors had less than a minute to answer the bell or the troubadours were high-tailing it on.

At one point, a van from a local nursing home, out viewing Christmas lights, slowed at a well-lit house down the street. The boys saw this as an opportunity not to be wasted and immediately positioned themselves on the snow-covered sidewalk to serenade the surprised group of senior saints.

I laughed and cried my way around the block, knowing I was witnessing the making of a treasured memory.

Each Christmas, I can hear the echoes of those brass instruments and little guys' voices up and down this street that has grown far too quiet. And it still makes me laugh and cry at the same time.

Oh, I hope you have stored up some laughter from this season! I hope you have echoes of joy that make you smile as you remember. And if you have, thank God for the precious gift of tendering your heart through the letting go and moving on.

Heavenly Father, I am so thankful that you know the fullness of a mother's heart at this time of year. In the tensions of planning for what is our current season while so many moments are filled with memories of times gone by, thank you for holding our tears and understanding the range of emotions. Father, help us to embrace and enjoy this current season. Help us to not hold too tightly the way things used to be. Teach us to be present in this year's celebration of the birth of Your Son.

Amen.

THE CHRISTMAS OF NO PANTS

Shelly

The excitement about spending Christmas with my family in Idaho would begin to bubble up in October of each year. The level of excitement when we started having kids made the anticipation greater. I couldn't wait to introduce my girls to the wonder of a white Christmas in the mountains of Idaho. I wanted them to fall backward into deep snow and swish their arms and legs in and out – creating tiny snow angels. I wanted them to zip on snowmobiles across fields of fresh snow and on trails once logging roads. I wanted to let them eat snow and build snow forts. I wanted them to sit next to a roaring fire, drinking hot chocolate while they watched snow quietly drift to the ground outside of my parents' mountain home. I wanted them to be around family and play with their cousins.

The excitement and anticipation were always *HIGH*.

When our oldest daughter was about two and a half years old, she rebelled against pants! That's right. Pants! She would NOT wear pants because, in her little mind, pants were for boys and dresses a "girl" and wore pants. And most of the "girls' in her life wore pants. And most of the "girls' in her life wore pants. But trying to argue with an irrational little toddler was futile, and since it wasn't life or death, I bought a lot of dresses.

The excitement and anticipation of planning for Christmas in a snowy, cold climate when we lived in hot and humid Houston had to be balanced with planning what we would wear. We didn't have money to buy snow clothes. When we went home, I still wore my ski outfit from high school, and my husband had some winter wear from his hunting days. When the kids came along, I gladly accepted hand-me-downs from my sister, who lived in Idaho. It worked out great – until sassy pants wouldn't wear pants.

The Christmas of No Pants lives in infamy even today – almost 30 years later. A few weeks ago, my dad brought it up again.

Let me explain. I loaded my suitcases with gifts and winter wear. I bought the thickest tights and leggings for my dresses-only daughter and the cutest pink mittens with feathers and curly ribbon on the back of the hands. She picked them out, and though they weren't practical, she was excited to wear them to play in the snow. I made sure my sister had snow clothes that would fit my daughter.

After spending Christmas in the city, thirteen of us—including my elderly grandfather—loaded up in cars and headed north to the mountains. When we arrived at the mountain home, the snow was deep, and my nephews wasted no time donning their snow clothes deep, and my nephews wasted no time donning their snow clothes and going out to play. I was excited to dress my daughter and send her out with the boys.

I fished the red ski bibs and gray boots from the bag my sister brought for me and walked into the living room, ready to dress my daughter. When she saw the pants in my hands, she shook her head, "NO!" She let me know the gray boots were not acceptable either.

I'm not sure why I thought the No-Pants rule didn't apply to snow clothes, but I did. This is when the ridiculousness began.

My husband and I began to reason with the pants-particular daughter. We made no dent in her resolve. Her cousins even begged her to go outside and build a snow fort with them. Nope!

We said things like, "There is no such thing as a snow dress" and "girls wear red snow pants." Nope!

That little girl refused to wear the snow pants for the next 24 hours. She spent long periods standing at the window watching her cousins play in the snow—with her pink mittens on. It broke my heart. I knew she would have so much fun playing in the snow.

We encouraged her. We reasoned with her. Then we got extra ridiculous and held her while trying to shove her feet into the gray boots. We are not proud of that, but it seemed reasonable at the time.

We acquiesced and agreed to let her wear her dress and double leggings if she wore snow boots. We were hoping she'd have fun, get cold, and decide to put on the red snow pants. Ridiculous reasoning, I know.

So, we held her still and put a gray boot on her little foot. As soon as we moved to the other foot, she kicked off the gray boot. We moved from foot to foot a few times until my grandfather wisely, gently said, "Let that baby go." We did.

We lost the battle. We were sad she couldn't play with her cousins in the snow, so we bargained on day number two of not playing in the snow. We struck up a deal with her that if we bought pink boots, she would wear the red pants. Off we dashed to the little mountain town in search of pink snow boots. And when I say little mountain town, I mean *little*. No Wal-Mart or Target. Just local, high-priced gear. If I would have bought the boots earlier while in the city, I could've saved a lot of money.

We found a pair of white boots with some pink on them. Boots we really couldn't afford. Since our pickings were slim, we hoped and prayed they would be acceptable to our No Pants girl.

We walked into the house with our bag, and I saw the look of relief on my parents' and grandfather's faces. They were undoubtedly relieved not to have to watch their sad little granddaughter long to go outside, or her parents wrestle her into pants and boots. It was not our best parenting moment, but we hoped the high-priced boots would compensate for our stupid thinking about forcing boots onto her feet.

The tension was thick as we waited for a positive response when we presented the pinkish boots. And we got it! She loved the snow boots and agreed to wear the red snow bibs. And she loved playing in the snow for hours with her cousins.

Those boots were worn by all three of our daughters and our two granddaughters, so we certainly got our money's worth out of the purchase.

We survived *The Christmas of No Pants* – barely!

I had visions of being tucked into a cozy mountain home, surrounded by all the people I love, and watching my daughter love the snowy activities like I did. But it didn't go as planned, and I was frustrated.

I'm sure Mary anticipated her son's birth very differently than how it happened. I imagine she planned to bring her son, Jesus, into the world surrounded by those she trusted and loved - not in a barn. Maybe she romanticized about relaxing during the days leading up to the birth instead of riding on a donkey for days.

I've learned to focus on what matters at Christmastime—the birth of Jesus and being surrounded by those I love. I pray that this Christmas season, you can focus on Jesus' birth and be surrounded by those you love.

THE 11ᵀᴴ HOUR

Laura

It doesn't matter how much time I have to complete a project, you can pretty much count on me not really kicking in until the deadline is breathing down my neck. It's not like I wasn't doing other things, mind you. I am always busy doing something. But working ahead… nope. This is not going to happen.

Each year as the final countdown days to Christmas loom before me, the reality is I usually have bedding fighting for space with table linens in the laundry room. The guest rooms are getting a once over while the sheets cycle through. Next there will be tablecloths and napkins to wash and press, if needed. And - oh yes - the table. Last minute craft projects cover all flat surfaces that do not have mixing bowls and ingredients on top of them.

I have lists on top of lists. There are ribbon shreds scattered on all levels of the house and a traveling roll of scotch tape that is as elusive as the address book. I have been eating a steady diet of cookies, chocolate, and leftover takeouts from various styrofoam containers, all washed down with massive amounts of coffee.

If you are like me, please remember to take time to breathe and refocus on why we celebrate. Keep balance and perspective as you finish up the last details. Remember to enjoy your friends and your family and your tasks and keep the season well.

Pep talk over, now pass me a cookie and help me find the scotch tape!

I kid.

Stop running around for just a minute and try this with me.

Slow down.

Take a deep breath.

Listen.

When the weariness from concerts, services, tasks, preparations and expectations melting into reality hit hard, I remind myself of these things:

♡ Gifts - Seriously?? Most likely everyone on our Christmas list already has more than enough. Our gifts are tokens of our love and/or appreciation. They should be FUN for you to purchase and FUN for them to open. If your kids/spouse/whoever does not get everything on their wish list then you have blessed them with the gift of not being over-indulged.

♡ Projects - It's ok if you didn't get them all finished. An IOU is much better than a cranky, overtired relative or friend who stayed up until 3 A.M. to finish a handmade gift. The recipient will have something to look forward to in January. And you, my friend, will have something to focus on besides taking down your tree.

♡ All those great ideas that were in your head and never came into fruition? Repeat after me...NO ONE KNOWS! You are the only one who knows all the cute and wonderful and awesome things you wanted to do that you never got around to doing. So just put those plans into some sort of mental file box and ....

LET

IT

GO.......

so you can just be filled with....

JOY

One year in the midst of the last minute whirlwind of pre-Christmas Eve frenzy, I was involved in a text thread with some friends about a prayer request. As the night grew late, I texted that I was heading to bed. In the morning when I looked at my phone I noticed Autocorrect had changed "heading" to "He King."

The Holy Spirit must have overridden technology to remind me of that as I woke on Christmas Eve morning.

He King.

Amen and amen.

Heavenly Father, You know that my heart desires to use this season to celebrate the birth of Your Son. You also know all the traditions I try to carry on for our family and the hopes I have to bring about a time of fellowship and joy and love in our home. Sometimes I get off track. Thank You for loving me and knowing my heart and true desires. Help me to rest in You. Help me to let go of perfectionism and comparison and expectations that lose sight of showing our family Your love and Your joy in this beautiful season. In Jesus' Name, Amen.

Made in the USA
Monee, IL
11 November 2024